FEARLESS
CONVERSATION™

IS GOD IN CONTROL OF MY LIFE?

DISCUSSIONS FROM JOSHUA, RUTH, AND ESTHER

PARTICIPANT GUIDE

Loveland, CO

Group

Real. **Bold.** Love.

Group resources really work!

This Group resource incorporates our R.E.A.L. approach to ministry. It reinforces a growing friendship with Jesus, encourages long-term learning, and results in life transformation, because it's:

Relational—Learner-to-learner interaction enhances learning and builds Christian friendships.

Experiential—What learners experience through discussion and action sticks with them up to 9 times longer than what they simply hear or read.

Applicable—The aim of Christian education is to equip learners to be both hearers and doers of God's Word.

Learner-based—Learners understand and retain more when the learning process takes into consideration how they learn best.

Fearless Conversation: Is God in Control of My Life?
Discussions from Joshua, Ruth, and Esther
Participant Guide

Visit our website: **group.com**

Fearless Conversation adult Sunday school curriculum is created by the amazing adult ministry team at Group. Contributing writers for this quarter are:

Lauren Bratten • Susan Lawrence • Larry Shallenberger • Amber Van Schooneveld • Jill Wuellner

Unless otherwise indicated, all Scripture quotations are taken from the *Holy Bible*, New International Version® NIV® Copyright © 1973, 1978, 1984, 2011 by Biblica, Inc.® Used by permission. All rights reserved worldwide.

ISBN 978-1-4707-1684-4

Printed in the United States of America

10 9 8 7 6 5 4 3 2 1   22 21 20 19 18 17 16 15

CONTENTS

HERE'S WHAT A LESSON LOOKS LIKE

Your leader will guide each lesson through four sections:

GREETING

Make new friends and start the conversation as the topic of the week is introduced.

GROUNDING

This is where you read the Scripture for the week. The Bible content is always provided here in the participant guide. After hearing God's Word read aloud, you'll have the opportunity to follow the inductive study method of writing down first responses, questions, thoughts, or ideas that are sparked by the Bible reading.

GRAPPLING

Here's where the conversation deepens. You'll find questions that are intentionally challenging to answer. These won't have easy answers and you won't have a fill-in-the-blank option. Everyone will wrestle with the questions that the lesson provides, as well as their own questions that they're wondering about. The leader will ask God to guide the conversation—and you can join in that prayer! Remember to treat others with respect during these conversations, even if you don't agree with them. Listen first. Speak second.

GROWING

Here's where the personal application comes in. You'll have the chance to reflect on what God's Word, as shared in this lesson, means to you for your own life and determine what your personal response is.

Throughout each lesson you'll also find two other helps:

BEHIND THE SCENES

These sections of commentary and notes from Bible scholars will give you additional context into history, language, culture, and other relevant information. You can read these sections ahead of time or during the lesson—whichever works best for you.

GOING DEEPER

These tips will help you be a great conversationalist. They remind you how to keep a conversation going, how to be a better listener, and how to be respectful even if you don't agree with someone.

FINAL TIP:

Have a sense of divine anticipation. Approach each class with a heart full of anticipation over what God might do that day. God is alive and present with you and your class. Always prepare by praying, asking God to help you see his hand at work in the conversation. Trust God to show up and show you and others in the class exactly where he wants the conversation to go!

FEARLESS CONVERSATION:
IS GOD IN CONTROL OF MY LIFE?

LESSON 1: DOES GOD EXPECT *ME* TO BE STRONG AND COURAGEOUS?

GREETING

What's one thing you're afraid of? Heights? The dark? Spiders? Something else?

The one word that comes to mind about a time I had to be strong and courageous is:

_____

GROUNDING

God's Word: Joshua 1:1-9

[1] After the death of Moses the servant of the Lord, the Lord said to Joshua son of Nun, Moses' aide: [2] "Moses my servant is dead. Now then, you and all these people, get ready to cross the Jordan River into the land I am about to give to them—to the Israelites. [3] I will give you every place where you set your foot, as I promised Moses. [4] Your territory will extend from the desert to Lebanon, and from the great river, the Euphrates—all the Hittite country—to the Mediterranean Sea in the west. [5] No one will be able to stand against you all the days of your life. As I was with Moses, so I will be with you; I will never leave you nor forsake you. [6] Be strong and courageous, because you will lead these people to inherit the land I swore to their ancestors to give them.

[7] "Be strong and very courageous. Be careful to obey all the law my servant Moses gave you; do not turn from it to the right or to the left, that you may be successful wherever you go. [8] Keep this Book of the Law always on your lips; meditate on it day and night, so that you may be careful to do everything written in it. Then you will be prosperous and successful. [9] Have I not commanded you? Be strong and courageous. Do not be afraid; do not be discouraged, for the Lord your God will be with you wherever you go."

BEHIND THE SCENES

The Hittite country mentioned in verse 4 doesn't refer to the Hittite Empire that was established in the region of modern Turkey around 1600 B.C. It's referring to the region of modern Syria, which was sometimes called "the land of the Hatti."

What are the first questions that come to mind? What words or phrases catch your attention in this passage?

Write down your thoughts and questions here.

BEHIND THE SCENES

Moses led the Israelites out of Egypt when Joshua was just a little boy, and Moses was the only leader the Israelites had ever known. Joshua, along with the older Israelites, would have experienced God's power firsthand. They witnessed the Red Sea part and passed through it. They had seen pillars of fire and cloud leading them. And they had miraculously found food, manna, to eat each day.

Although the older Israelites were born and lived as slaves in Egypt, those less than 40 years old had only known an existence of wandering through the desert as nomads. After 40 years of wandering, they were finally going to their promised home.

GRAPPLING

GOING DEEPER

You can help others in your group go deeper by listening with your full attention and by asking questions as others share. Saying "I wonder about what you just said. Tell me more!" will help people know you care about what they're saying and want them to open up more.

PARTICIPANT GUIDE

What if you were the Israelites? You used to be slaves. You've been wandering in the desert for decades. And now God wants you to enter an unknown land and conquer the people there. What would your thoughts and feelings be?

In verse 9, God promises that "the Lord your God will be with you wherever you go." What do you think it means that God was with the Israelites? What does it mean, practically, that God is with us? How might that have a bearing on being strong and courageous?

BEHIND THE SCENES

In Joshua 1:9, God promised he would be with the Israelites. Jesus promised his disciples something similar in Matthew 28:20: "And surely I am with you always, to the very end of the age."

What significance (if any) might there be in the fact that God's words, "Be strong and courageous," are stated three times? What would it have meant to Joshua and the people of Israel given their situation? What connections might there be between these commands and the other two commands in this passage?

BEHIND THE SCENES

In Joshua 1:2-4, the word "you" is plural, whereas "you" in verses 5-9 is singular. Bible commentators theorize that verses 2-4 were directed at the Israelite nation, while verses 5-9 were directed at Joshua.

Joshua received two promises and three commandments from God. The promises are: 1) no one will be able to stand against him; 2) the Lord will be with him. The first command (which is repeated three times!) is to be strong and courageous. The second command is to obey the Law, and the third is to meditate on the Law day and night.

INTERESTING THOUGHTS SPARKED BY OTHERS IN MY GROUP:

BEHIND THE SCENES

God had first promised land to the Israelites hundreds of years earlier through Abraham, the father of the Israelite nation: "The Lord appeared to Abram and said, 'To your offspring I will give this land.'" (Genesis 12:7). God repeated this promise to Abraham in Genesis 13:14-15 and 15:7.

So why did Abraham's descendants have to wait hundreds of years to get the land? Genesis 15:16 says, "In the fourth generation your descendants will come back here, for the sin of the Amorites has not yet reached its full measure." God knew that the people living in this land were going to commit sins so egregious that the culture needed to end.

GROWING

Is there a situation in your life in which you think God is asking you to be strong and courageous? What possible effects could this have on God's mission or purposes in the world?

Write your thoughts here.

LESSON 2: WHY ARE IMPERFECT PEOPLE PART OF GOD'S PLAN?

GREETING

You have run out of gas on a deserted road. A stranger has offered to drive to a gas station 10 minutes away and bring back some gas for your car. If you had no other choice, which of the following persons would you most likely agree to let them help you?

A. A greasy-haired, bling-wearing used-car salesman

B. A meth-addled woman of uncertain age

C. A pot-bellied, cigar-smoking U.S. Congressman

D. A profanity-spewing goth girl covered with tattoos and piercings

E. A bearded, swarthy man speaking with a heavy foreign accent

GROUNDING

BEHIND THE SCENES

Jericho was a city-state in Canaan with its own king. The city covered an area of about 8 or 9 acres. Based on evidence found, some archaeologists believe the city had double walls about 15 feet apart protecting the city.

God's Word: Joshua 2:1-21

[1] Then Joshua son of Nun secretly sent two spies from Shittim. "Go, look over the land," he said, "especially Jericho." So they went and entered the house of a prostitute named Rahab and stayed there.

[2] The king of Jericho was told, "Look, some of the Israelites have come here tonight to spy out the land." [3] So the king of Jericho sent this message to Rahab: "Bring out the men who came to you and entered your house, because they have come to spy out the whole land."

[4] But the woman had taken the two men and hidden them. She said, "Yes, the men came to me, but I did not know where they had come from. [5] At dusk, when it was time to close the city gate, they left. I don't know which way they went. Go after them quickly. You may catch up with them." [6] (But she had taken them up to the roof and hidden them under the stalks of flax she had laid out on the roof.) [7] So the men set out in pursuit of the spies on the road that leads to the fords of the Jordan, and as soon as the pursuers had gone out, the gate was shut.

[8] Before the spies lay down for the night, she went up on the roof [9] and said to them, "I know that the Lord has given you this land and that a great fear of you has fallen on us, so that all who live in this country are melting in fear because of you. [10] We have heard how the Lord dried

PARTICIPANT GUIDE

up the water of the Red Sea for you when you came out of Egypt, and what you did to Sihon and Og, the two kings of the Amorites east of the Jordan, whom you completely destroyed. [11] When we heard of it, our hearts melted in fear and everyone's courage failed because of you, for the Lord your God is God in heaven above and on the earth below.

[12] "Now then, please swear to me by the Lord that you will show kindness to my family, because I have shown kindness to you. Give me a sure sign [13] that you will spare the lives of my father and mother, my brothers and sisters, and all who belong to them—and that you will save us from death."

[14] "Our lives for your lives!" the men assured her. "If you don't tell what we are doing, we will treat you kindly and faithfully when the Lord gives us the land."

[15] So she let them down by a rope through the window, for the house she lived in was part of the city wall. [16] She said to them, "Go to the hills so the pursuers will not find you. Hide yourselves there three days until they return, and then go on your way."

[17] Now the men had said to her, "This oath you made us swear will not be binding on us [18] unless, when we enter the land, you have tied this scarlet cord in the window through which you let us down, and unless you have brought your father and mother, your brothers and all your family into your house. [19] If any of them go outside your house into the street, their blood will be on their own heads; we will not be responsible. As for those who are in the house with you, their blood will be on our head if a hand is laid on them. [20] But if you tell what we are doing, we will be released from the oath you made us swear."

[21] "Agreed," she replied. "Let it be as you say."

So she sent them away, and they departed. And she tied the scarlet cord in the window.

What questions do you have? What caught your attention?

Write down those initial thoughts and questions here.

BEHIND THE SCENES

The Hebrew word in the book of Joshua used to describe Rahab could mean "innkeeper." But in the New Testament, the writers of James 2:25 and Hebrews 11:31 use the Greek word that explicitly means "prostitute."

Rahab could have been a common prostitute or a prostitute in the fertility cult, which was an important aspect of Canaanite religion. Whatever the precise nature of her occupation, two strange men could enter her household without looking as conspicuous as they would at other households.

GRAPPLING

GOING DEEPER

Be sensitive to the various backgrounds of the people in your group. Some may have very different experiences from you, but God just may use them to teach you something big!

The Israelite spies received help from a surprising source. What do you think is most scandalous about Rahab? Her gender? (Female in a male-centric culture.) Her occupation? (Prostitute.) Her ethnic identity? (Canaanite.) Her society's religious practices? (Worship of the pagan god Baal.) Others?

Rahab is praised in Hebrews 11 for her great faith. What did Rahab *say* in Joshua 2 to make the spies trust her and justify her place in the Hebrews' list of heroes of the faith?

Rahab is praised in James 2 for her acts of faith. What did Rahab *do* in Joshua 2 to make the spies trust her and justify James' mention of her?

BEHIND THE SCENES

Hebrews 11 is known as the Faith Hall of Fame, listing people throughout the Bible who have shown great faith in God. Rahab is one of those listed—one of only two women! (The other is Sarah, the wife of Abraham, who is the father of the Israelite people.)

In James 2:25, Rahab is mentioned as an example of someone whose faith is proven by her deeds. The other person in this chapter praised for great faith is Abraham. James says that both were considered righteous because of their faith that led to deeds.

Why do you think Rahab helped the Israelites? What clues in the passage tell you this?

What does Joshua 2 say to you about how God works through people to accomplish his purposes in the world?

INTERESTING THOUGHTS SPARKED BY OTHERS
IN MY GROUP:

BEHIND THE SCENES

In Matthew 1:5 we read something pretty amazing. In the list of Jesus' genealogy, Rahab is listed as an ancestor of Jesus! Rahab is the grandmother of Boaz—the great and honorable man we read of in the book of Ruth who was the great-grandfather of King David! Joseph, Jesus' earthly father, came from the lineage of David.

GROWING

Who are our "Rahabs" today? Who are people—Christian or not—through whom God is working?

Write your ideas here.

Put yourself in Rahab's place and in the Israelite spies' place. What does Joshua 2 say to you about your role in God's mission?

- **As Rahab, what does this story tell you about God's willingness to accept and use anyone, regardless of background, who wants to serve God?**

   Record those ideas here.

- **As the Israelite spies, what have you learned about recognizing God's grace at work in the world through people you don't expect—and accepting them?**

   Write your thoughts here.

PARTICIPANT GUIDE

LESSON 3: WHY DOES GOD'S PLAN SEEM SO COMPLICATED?

GREETING

What's a set of directions your parents gave you that seemed unnecessary then but makes sense now?

Why don't children just naturally appreciate their parents' motives when it comes to the instructions they give?

What are some current situations—whether at home, work, or church—in which you find yourself having to follow someone's plan that feels unnecessarily complicated? How does that typically make you feel?

In general, how do you tend to respond when you find yourself in these situations?

GROUNDING

God's Word: Joshua 6:1-21

[1] Now the gates of Jericho were securely barred because of the Israelites. No one went out and no one came in.

[2] Then the Lord said to Joshua, "See, I have delivered Jericho into your hands, along with its king and its fighting men. [3] March around the city once with all the armed men. Do this for six days. [4] Have seven priests carry trumpets of rams' horns in front of the ark. On the seventh day, march around the city seven times, with the priests blowing the trumpets. [5] When you hear them sound a long blast on the trumpets, have the whole army give a loud shout; then the wall of the city will collapse and the army will go up, everyone straight in."

▼

6 So Joshua son of Nun called the priests and said to them, "Take up the ark of the covenant of the Lord and have seven priests carry trumpets in front of it." 7 And he ordered the army, "Advance! March around the city, with an armed guard going ahead of the ark of the Lord."

8 When Joshua had spoken to the people, the seven priests carrying the seven trumpets before the Lord went forward, blowing their trumpets, and the ark of the Lord's covenant followed them. 9 The armed guard marched ahead of the priests who blew the trumpets, and the rear guard followed the ark. All this time the trumpets were sounding. 10 But Joshua had commanded the army, "Do not give a war cry, do not raise your voices, do not say a word until the day I tell you to shout. Then shout!" 11 So he had the ark of the Lord carried around the city, circling it once. Then the army returned to camp and spent the night there.

12 Joshua got up early the next morning and the priests took up the ark of the Lord. 13 The seven priests carrying the seven trumpets went forward, marching before the ark of the Lord and blowing the trumpets. The armed men went ahead of them and the rear guard followed the ark of the Lord, while the trumpets kept sounding. 14 So on the second day they marched around the city once and returned to the camp. They did this for six days.

15 On the seventh day, they got up at daybreak and marched around the city seven times in the same manner, except that on that day they circled the city seven times. 16 The seventh time around, when the priests sounded the trumpet blast, Joshua commanded the army, "Shout! For the Lord has given you the city! 17 The city and all that is in it are to be devoted to the Lord. Only Rahab the prostitute and all who are with her in her house shall be spared, because she hid the spies we sent. 18 But keep away from the devoted things, so that you will not bring about your own destruction by taking any of them. Otherwise you will make the camp of Israel liable to destruction and bring trouble on it. 19 All the silver and gold and the articles of bronze and iron are sacred to the Lord and must go into his treasury."

20 When the trumpets sounded, the army shouted, and at the sound of the trumpet, when the men gave a loud shout, the wall collapsed; so

everyone charged straight in, and they took the city. [21] They devoted the city to the Lord and destroyed with the sword every living thing in it— men and women, young and old, cattle, sheep and donkeys.

What are the first questions that come to mind about this passage? What jumps off the page at you?

Record your initial thoughts and questions here.

BEHIND THE SCENES

The siege of Jericho is the first recorded military campaign recorded in the book of Joshua. Jericho was an important Canaanite military garrison positioned just west of the Jordan River. Taking the outpost had strategic importance for Israel. It was the first step toward dividing Canaan in half. Once the center of the territory was held, strategic supply lines would be cut off, allowing the 12 tribes a strong position from which to take the rest of the country. The problem was that whatever military knowledge the 12 tribes possessed had been forgotten during their 400 years of slavery in Egypt. Jericho's closed gates presented an obstacle that Israel was unprepared to overcome.

The armies of Israel would eventually need to draw their swords and engage in combat. However, God had something different in mind for their first battle. God instructed that the army should silently circle the walled city once each day for six days. A small contingent of priests, carrying trumpets and the Ark of the Covenant, would lead this strange procession. On the seventh day, after completing seven laps around the city, the priests were to blow their trumpets, accompanied by loud shouts from the army. God promised the walls of the city would fall to the ground.

GRAPPLING

How do you think Joshua felt as he prepared to relay God's instructions to the Israelites?

The number seven was significant in the creation account in Genesis 1. What might God have been communicating to Israel by incorporating that number into his complicated instructions to Israel?

BEHIND THE SCENES

During the conquest of Canaan, the vanquished cities were often placed under "the ban." This meant it was devoted to God alone, and no human could lay claim to it. As with sacrificial offerings, things devoted to God were completely destroyed, usually by burning. This practice had the additional benefit of avoiding squabbles over plunder. No individual Israelite would get rich from the spoils of war. When applied to material goods or even livestock, this practice is understandable to modern readers, although it may seem a bit wasteful. However, when vanquished *people* are included in the ban, the morality of the practice moves from being questionable to downright objectionable.

Theologically, the ban was necessary because the pagan nations were under God's judgment for their pagan worship practices, which included fertility orgies and child sacrifice. If Israel were to survive to carry out its mission to bless the entire world as God told Abraham in Genesis 12, it could not be contaminated by pagan religious practices. In the brutal culture of the Ancient Near East, contamination could be eliminated only through extreme means.

Despite this rationale, modern readers may still struggle with God's command to kill all the women and children of Jericho. Here it might be helpful to note that Jericho was a military garrison, and there is no archeological evidence that a civilian population ever lived there. In his book *Is God a Moral Monster?*, biblical scholar Paul Copan argues that the orders to kill the young, the old, and the women was stock language in the Ancient Middle East. It was the typical bravado of military commanders and was used even if women and children didn't live in the vicinity. Copan states that he believes Jericho and Ai were used for "government buildings and operations, while the rest of the people (including women and children) lived in the surrounding countryside."

What effect do you think the supernatural fall of Jericho had on the other Canaanite cities?

How would this have worked to Israel's advantage throughout the rest of their conquest of Canaan?

INTERESTING THOUGHTS SPARKED BY OTHERS IN MY GROUP:

GOING DEEPER

Some of your fellow participants may share personal experiences in which they don't understand God's plan for them. Important: It's not your place or job to supply the reasons. God often doesn't reveal his reasons on this side of heaven. When he does, it's usually long after the confusing situation has passed. Instead, empathize with how frustrating their situation is and express confidence that they can trust God even if they can't understand him now.

What did Joshua and the people of Israel want to accomplish by attacking Jericho?

What overriding objective does it appear God had for this military operation? (What did God want to teach Israel?)

GROWING

Think about a time in the past when God's plans seemed confusing to you. Looking back, what do you think God was trying to accomplish?

Write your reflections here.

Where does God's plan seem confusing to you now? What do you know about God that allows you to live with this confusion?

Write your thoughts here.

LESSON 4: HOW DOES MY SIN IMPACT OTHERS?

GREETING

In your small group, come up with two or three protective safeguards appropriate for each "community" listed below. Then come up with a consequence or penalty that community could impose on those who violate their safeguards.

A HOCKEY TEAM

Safeguards:

Consequence or Penalty:

A WEIGHT-LOSS SUPPORT GROUP

Safeguards:

Consequence or Penalty:

A BOWLING LEAGUE

Safeguards:

Consequence or Penalty:

A CABIN FULL OF DEER HUNTERS

Safeguards:

Consequence or Penalty:

A SCHOOL CLASSROOM

Safeguards:

Consequence or Penalty:

GROUNDING

BEHIND THE SCENES

The idea that God would command his people to kill innocent people as part of their warfare is difficult for modern readers to stomach. Refer to the "Behind the Scenes" box in the "Grappling" section of Lesson 3 for more information about "the ban," which may help your class come to terms with this difficult commandment.

God's Word: Joshua 7:1, 19-26

[1] But the Israelites were unfaithful in regard to the devoted things; Achan son of Karmi, the son of Zimri, the son of Zerah, of the tribe of Judah, took some of them. So the Lord's anger burned against Israel.

[19] Then Joshua said to Achan, "My son, give glory to the Lord, the God of Israel, and honor him. Tell me what you have done; do not hide it from me."

[20] Achan replied, "It is true! I have sinned against the Lord, the God of Israel. This is what I have done: [21] When I saw in the plunder a beautiful robe from Babylonia, two hundred shekels of silver and a bar of gold weighing fifty shekels, I coveted them and took them. They are hidden in the ground inside my tent, with the silver underneath."

[22] So Joshua sent messengers, and they ran to the tent, and there it was, hidden in his tent, with the silver underneath. [23] They took the things from the tent, brought them to Joshua and all the Israelites and spread them out before the Lord.

[24] Then Joshua, together with all Israel, took Achan son of Zerah, the silver, the robe, the gold bar, his sons and daughters, his cattle, donkeys and sheep, his tent and all that he had, to the Valley of Achor. [25] Joshua said, "Why have you brought this trouble on us? The Lord will bring trouble on you today."

Then all Israel stoned him, and after they had stoned the rest, they burned them. [26] Over Achan they heaped up a large pile of rocks, which remains to this day. Then the Lord turned from his fierce anger. Therefore that place has been called the Valley of Achor ever since.

What went through your mind as we read this account? How do you feel about God's reaction to Achan's sin? What questions do you have?

Write your observations and questions here.

BEHIND THE SCENES

The chapter opens with the reader being given an important piece of information that Joshua isn't privy to at the beginning of the story. Achan has violated the ban by stealing a robe, a bar of gold, and 200 coins during the conquest of Jericho. God doesn't view this as the offense of a single individual, but of the whole nation. God made his covenant with a community and not an individual person. So when one member of that community violated that covenant, it was as if the entire community violated the agreement. In this story, individual and corporate responsibilities go hand-in-hand. All of Israel is caught up in the effects of Achan's sin. But it's Achan who is isolated as the guilty party.

GRAPPLING

Consider God's response to Achan's sin. Do you think the punishment fit the crime? Why do you think that?

If the entire nation of Israel is guilty of disobedience, why did God not destroy them all?

Notice that Joshua 7:1 is built like a sandwich: the focus of the first and last phrases is the nation of Israel. In the middle, the focus narrows down to Achan. How can this help us interpret verses 19-26?

After discussing this story, can you see any justification for God's punishment of Achan and his family?

BEHIND THE SCENES

Bible scholars point out that the way sin is viewed in this passage is far different from how sin was viewed by neighboring nations. For example, in Egypt, where the Israelites had been for 400 years, sin was viewed merely as a slight disruption of the cosmic order. However, in this chapter, sin is personal. Achan, first and foremost, sinned against God himself. But his sin also had a relational impact on his family, his clan, his tribe, and his nation. We see this same relational element of sin in the account of the Fall. Adam and Eve's sin alienated them from God and also placed a relational wedge between each other and between themselves and the rest of God's creation. The biblical view of sin is not the breaking of an impersonal list of rules. Instead, we are breaking the relational bond that connects us to God, each other, and our world.

INTERESTING THOUGHTS SPARKED BY OTHERS
IN MY GROUP:

GROWING

The Bible views Achan's disobedience as a community problem. How does this compare with how we view sin in our more individualistic culture? What are some examples?

Record those thoughts here.

GOING DEEPER

The topic of sin and its consequences can be sensitive and painful for some people—perhaps even you. It's not fun to recall our past weaknesses and mistakes. So, while we don't want to avoid the issue altogether, do make a conscious effort to be gentle and kind to others (and yourself) in your discussions. Above all, remember that God's grace is more powerful than our sins and the effects of those sins.

What are some current examples in which you can imagine the sins of one person having a negative impact on others?

Write those ideas here.

How does your relationship with God affect other people near to you? Is the impact positive or otherwise?

Record your thoughts here.

Think about your most recent interpersonal conflict. What impact has your conflict had on people other than yourself and the person with whom you are in conflict?

Write your ideas here.

What can you do to help heal or reconcile relationships that became collateral damage in these conflicts?

Write your thoughts here.

LESSON 5: HOW CAN WE LIVE WITH INTEGRITY IN A WORLD THAT DOESN'T?

GREETING

Think about a time when you conducted personal or professional business with people whom you weren't fully able to trust. How did you feel in that situation? Why?

What are some strategies you've used to protect yourself when you're with people you aren't fully able to trust?

GOING DEEPER

You can help others in your group go deeper by listening with your full attention and by asking questions as others share. Saying "I wonder about what you just said. Tell me more!" will help people know you care about what they're saying and want them to open up more.

GROUNDING

BEHIND THE SCENES

The Bible passage for this lesson uses some terms interchangeably, which could lead to confusion. The land of Canaan was inhabited by numerous people groups who shared similar language, religion, and other cultural aspects. These people groups were similar to the Israelite tribes, who lived in a certain region. Within these regions were independent city-states ruled by a "king," who was more like a clan chieftain. One of these tribal groups was the Hivites, who banded together with some other groups to oppose Joshua and the Israelites (Joshua 9:1-2, 7).

Among the Hivites were the Gibeonites, who included the people who lived in the city of Gibeon but also smaller groups nearby who lived in three other towns (9:17). Scholars estimate that Gibeon was roughly 19 miles from the Israelite camp at Gilgal. There was no way Israel would knowingly enter into a treaty with a potential enemy so close to their base of operations. Joshua 9:3-21 tells how the Gibeonites (who are also called Hivites in this passage) managed to win a peace treaty with Israel.

God's Word: Joshua 9:3-21

³ However, when the people of Gibeon heard what Joshua had done to Jericho and Ai, ⁴ they resorted to a ruse: They went as a delegation whose donkeys were loaded with worn-out sacks and old wineskins, cracked and mended. ⁵ They put worn and patched sandals on their feet and wore old clothes. All the bread of their food supply was dry and moldy. ⁶ Then they went to Joshua in the camp at Gilgal and said to him and the Israelites, "We have come from a distant country; make a treaty with us."

⁷ The Israelites said to the Hivites, "But perhaps you live near us, so how can we make a treaty with you?"

⁸ "We are your servants," they said to Joshua.

But Joshua asked, "Who are you and where do you come from?"

⁹ They answered: "Your servants have come from a very distant country because of the fame of the Lord your God. For we have heard reports of him: all that he did in Egypt, ¹⁰ and all that he did to the two kings of the Amorites east of the Jordan—Sihon king of Heshbon, and Og king of Bashan, who reigned in Ashtaroth. ¹¹ And our elders and all those living in our country said to us, 'Take provisions for your journey; go and meet them and say to them, "We are your servants; make a treaty with us."' ¹² This bread of ours was warm when we packed it at home on the day we left to come to you. But now see how dry and moldy it is. ¹³ And these wineskins that we filled were new, but see how cracked they are. And our clothes and sandals are worn out by the very long journey."

¹⁴ The Israelites sampled their provisions but did not inquire of the Lord. ¹⁵ Then Joshua made a treaty of peace with them to let them live, and the leaders of the assembly ratified it by oath.

¹⁶ Three days after they made the treaty with the Gibeonites, the Israelites heard that they were neighbors, living near them. ¹⁷ So the

PARTICIPANT GUIDE

Israelites set out and on the third day came to their cities: Gibeon, Kephirah, Beeroth and Kiriath Jearim. [18] But the Israelites did not attack them, because the leaders of the assembly had sworn an oath to them by the Lord, the God of Israel.

The whole assembly grumbled against the leaders, [19] but all the leaders answered, "We have given them our oath by the Lord, the God of Israel, and we cannot touch them now. [20] This is what we will do to them: We will let them live, so that God's wrath will not fall on us for breaking the oath we swore to them." [21] They continued, "Let them live, but let them be woodcutters and water carriers in the service of the whole assembly." So the leaders' promise to them was kept.

What went through your mind as you read this account? What impressions of Joshua did you get? Is there something here you question?

Write down your initial thoughts and questions here.

BEHIND THE SCENES

The narrator of the book of Joshua doesn't fault Joshua for negotiating with the Gibeonites. In fact, in Deuteronomy 20:10-15, while prescribing the terms of "the ban," God allowed Israel to make treaties with far-off nations. But the narrator does note that Israel was guilty of not consulting God. It implies that the Israelite tribal leaders fell for the Gibeonites' flattery—the suggestion that Israel's fame in battle, and by extension Joshua's, had reached them in their "very distant country" (Joshua 9:6, 9). Joshua may have been so taken with a nation begging for peace at the very beginning of his campaign that he overlooked how suspicious it was that a "very distant country" was seeking to negotiate peace with Israel.

GRAPPLING

What do you think about the Gibeonites' tactics in making a peace treaty with Israel? What would you do if you were in their place? What if you were in Joshua's place?

The Gibeonites negotiated in bad faith. Why didn't Joshua and the Israelite leaders argue that their covenant with the Gibeonites wasn't valid?

The people were frustrated with Israel's leadership with the Gibeonites in the moment. But how might the leaders' response have earned the people's respect in the long term? Can you think of any current examples of people—either from current events or your own life—who have made mistakes but earned the respect of others by taking responsibility for those shortcomings?

BEHIND THE SCENES

It's interesting to note that even though the leaders of Israel were duped by the Gibeonites, they were adamant about owning their responsibility in the situation. When the people discovered the situation and began to grumble, the leaders took the blame. They didn't blame Joshua or point out how they initially challenged their general. The leaders also didn't acquiesce to the people's demands to attack the Gibeonites. They had made a vow before God with the Gibeonites and knew they were obligated to keep it. Instead of sacrificing their integrity, they settled for the best outcome they could find within the terms of their vows.

INTERESTING THOUGHTS SPARKED BY OTHERS
IN MY GROUP:

GROWING

Looking at all the characters in this story, what are some principles we might deduce from this text that would help us maintain our integrity as we deal with people who lack integrity?

Write your ideas here.

BEHIND THE SCENES

It's important to note that the Gibeonites' trickery was not without consequence. This once proud nation of warriors found themselves reduced to being servants of the Israelites. Joshua conscripted them to be Israel's wood cutters and water carriers. More than that, Joshua assigned them these roles in order to build altars constructed in the honor of the God of Israel (Joshua 9:23). It's ironic: The Gibeonites ended up becoming the servants of the very people they hoped to avoid; and the Israelites, whom God had freed from Egyptian building projects, now had another people serving them in a similar capacity.

Is there an area of your life in which you find you're having to deal with people who lack integrity in their dealings with others? What would it look like for you to depend on God in those circumstances?

Write your thoughts here.

Is there an area in your life in which you've been less than honest with others? What do you need to do to make that relationship right?

Write your reflections here.

LESSON 6: WHY WOULD GOD PROTECT LAWBREAKERS?

GREETING

Meet with three or four other people and come up with a group consensus as to why the laws listed below would ever have been created.

- In Farmington, Connecticut, cows have the same rights on the roads as do motorists.

- In North Dakota, it's illegal to serve beer and pretzels together.

- In Orlando, Florida, if you tether your elephant to a parking meter you must pay the meter fare, just as if you were parking a car.

- In Winona Lake, Wisconsin, it is illegal to eat ice cream at a counter on Sunday.

- In Normal, Oklahoma, you may not tease dogs by making ugly faces at them.

- In Memphis, Tennessee, a woman may only drive a car if there is a man with a red flag in front of the car warning the other people on the road.

• **What does this activity tell you about the nature of some of our laws and our changing times?**

BEHIND THE SCENES

Yes, the Bible is our guide for life and faith, but it's important to remember that each book had a unique original audience that was *not* us. When we read the laws found in the first five books of the Bible, it's important to remember God was giving laws to an ancient nation, located in a certain time, with a different culture and different social needs.

Some of the laws were ceremonial—instructions for how the priesthood and sacrificial systems were to work. Some laws were civil—specific instructions for that ancient government. Other laws are timeless guidelines for ethical and moral behavior. A good rule of thumb for knowing which laws still apply today is to see which ones were repeated by Jesus and/or the disciples and apostles in the New Testament. Not surprisingly, every one of the Ten Commandments was reaffirmed in the New Testament writings.

GROUNDING

God's Word: Joshua 20:1-9

[1] Then the Lord said to Joshua: [2] "Tell the Israelites to designate the cities of refuge, as I instructed you through Moses, [3] so that anyone who kills a person accidentally and unintentionally may flee there and find protection from the avenger of blood. [4] When they flee to one of these cities, they are to stand in the entrance of the city gate and state their case before the elders of that city. Then the elders are to admit the fugitive into their city and provide a place to live among them. [5] If the avenger of blood comes in pursuit, the elders must not surrender the fugitive, because the fugitive killed their neighbor unintentionally and without malice aforethought. [6] They are to stay in that city until they have stood trial before the assembly and until the death of the high priest who is serving at that time. Then they may go back to their own home in the town from which they fled."

[7] So they set apart Kedesh in Galilee in the hill country of Naphtali, Shechem in the hill country of Ephraim, and Kiriath Arba (that is, Hebron) in the hill country of Judah. [8] East of the Jordan (on the other side from Jericho) they designated Bezer in the wilderness on the plateau in the tribe of Reuben, Ramoth in Gilead in the tribe of Gad, and Golan in Bashan in the tribe of Manasseh. [9] Any of the Israelites or any foreigner residing among them who killed someone accidentally could flee to these designated cities and not be killed by the avenger of blood prior to standing trial before the assembly.

What went through your mind as you read this account? What impressions or questions do you have?

Write down your initial thoughts and questions here.

BEHIND THE SCENES

The idea of a city of refuge wasn't new to Joshua. God had already spoken to Moses regarding the matter (Numbers 35; Deuteronomy 19), but now that the conquest of the Promised Land was nearing its completion, it was time for Israel to obey God's mandate. The cities of refuge were intended for individuals who had killed unintentionally and without premeditation. Such persons would be protected there from angry family members of the deceased. The perpetrator was assigned a place to live within the city until the elders could convene a trial to determine if the killing truly was accidental. If it was determined that the killing was intentional, the killer would be handed over for execution. However, if the death was caused by accident, the person was permitted to live, but only within the walls of the city. In part, this served as a penalty for killing another person. But it was also a form of mercy, since the family of the deceased was not permitted to enter the city to get retribution for their loved one's death.

GRAPPLING

BEHIND THE SCENES

In addition to Joshua 20, passages in Numbers 35 and Deuteronomy 19 also make reference to "the avenger of blood." In this period of Israel's society, a kinsman of someone who was killed had a responsibility to seek justice for his fallen relative—thus the term "avenger of blood." The avenger of blood wasn't expected to examine the killer's motive (or lack of one in the case of an accident); he was only to bring justice in the form of retribution. However, in the case of an accidental killing, God prescribed cities of refuge so that an inadvertent slayer was safe from the avenger of blood, and the avenger would have time to gain perspective on his tragic but accidental loss.

What kinds of problems or excesses can you foresee in a "blood avenger" system like this, where family members were empowered to work their own brand of justice?

God wanted Israel's judges to consider the offenders' motives as well as actions before delivering a verdict. What does this tell you about God's nature?

What does the establishment of cities of refuge tell you about God's perspective on justice and the value of human life?

GOING DEEPER

The establishment of cities of refuge was basically a method of dealing with crime and punishment in Old Testament Israel. This lesson could easily lead into discussions about our criminal justice system, immigration, and the concepts of revenge, retribution, and amnesty—all hot-button topics! Fearless conversation does not skirt difficult subjects, but it addresses them with humble listening, careful wording, and respect for others' opinions. If you keep your focus on those qualities, your discussion won't erode into a debate that has winners and losers, but will be enlightening and constructive for everyone.

GROWING

Does the contemporary church have any comparable function to the cities of refuge? If so, how might churches be a place of refuge/asylum/sanctuary?

Write those ideas here.

If we show mercy to someone who inadvertently wrongs us, how might their opinion of God change? What price would we need to pay to show that mercy?

Write you thoughts here.

Where is God calling you to show mercy to someone who has offended you?

Write your reflections here.

Do you know of anyone whom you have inadvertently hurt or offended? What do you need from God to help you make things right with the other person?

Write your thoughts here.

LESSON 7: HOW DO MY RELATIONSHIPS AFFECT MY WALK WITH GOD?

GREETING

Who is one person you have a relationship with—other than a spouse or parent—who has had a major positive impact on your walk with God?

How do you think your life might have been different if you had never met that person?

What are some qualities and characteristics you would want your children (or nephews/nieces or hypothetical children) to consider when choosing a future spouse?

PARTICIPANT GUIDE

GROUNDING

BEHIND THE SCENES

The Scripture for this lesson focuses on some of the final words of the great leader Joshua. He was Moses' trusted aide and one of the scouts Moses sent into the Promised Land to see what the Israelites were up against. From the beginning of the conquest, he believed God would give the Israelites the land of Canaan. Joshua's long and outstanding history with the Israelites would have made him one of the most respected people in the community. Surely the people and leaders of Israel were hanging on Joshua's every word as he passed on his final advice and desires.

God's Word: Joshua 23:6-16

6 "Be very strong; be careful to obey all that is written in the Book of the Law of Moses, without turning aside to the right or to the left. 7 Do not associate with these nations that remain among you; do not invoke the names of their gods or swear by them. You must not serve them or bow down to them. 8 But you are to hold fast to the Lord your God, as you have until now.

9 "The Lord has driven out before you great and powerful nations; to this day no one has been able to withstand you. 10 One of you routs a thousand, because the Lord your God fights for you, just as he promised. 11 So be very careful to love the Lord your God.

12 "But if you turn away and ally yourselves with the survivors of these nations that remain among you and if you intermarry with them and associate with them, 13 then you may be sure that the Lord your God will no longer drive out these nations before you. Instead, they will become snares and traps for you, whips on your backs and thorns in ▶

your eyes, until you perish from this good land, which the Lord your God has given you.

[14] "Now I am about to go the way of all the earth. You know with all your heart and soul that not one of all the good promises the Lord your God gave you has failed. Every promise has been fulfilled; not one has failed. [15] But just as all the good things the Lord your God has promised you have come to you, so he will bring on you all the evil things he has threatened, until the Lord your God has destroyed you from this good land he has given you. [16] If you violate the covenant of the Lord your God, which he commanded you, and go and serve other gods and bow down to them, the Lord's anger will burn against you, and you will quickly perish from the good land he has given you."

What went through your mind as you read this account? How do you feel about Joshua's final instructions to the Israelites?

Write your initial thoughts and questions here.

GRAPPLING

BEHIND THE SCENES

Joshua's speeches from chapters 23 and 24 are very reminiscent of suzerainty treaties. These treaties were common in nearby cultures, such as the Hittites, and cultures found in Mesopotamia, Syria, and Egypt. A suzerainty treaty was a treaty between the suzerain, or feudal lord, and the vassals, or subjects. God's relationship with the Israelites can be compared to this suzerain-vassal relationship. The similarities between the book of Deuteronomy and our passage from Joshua and the suzerainty treaties from nearby cultures at the time (the fourteenth through thirteenth century B.C.) reinforce the reliability of the Bible. Later treaties from the eighth through seventh centuries focus solely on the curses that would fall on a people if they didn't follow the contract. Instead, we see Joshua emphasize the blessings of following the Lord's commands as well as warning of the curses.

Why would Joshua be so worried the Israelites would be tempted to worship other gods after all God had done for them?

Besides the obvious answer of God's blessing or lack of blessing, what were some possible *benefits* for the Israelites in following God's instructions?

What were some possible consequences of the Israelites disobeying God and marrying the people of other nations?

BEHIND THE SCENES

Joshua's instructions in our passage reveal the Canaanite people continued to live around and even among the Israelites, even after the conquest. This reaffirms the point made in previous lessons that the language of total destruction and slaughter found in Joshua and other parts of the Old Testament may not have applied to the entire Canaanite population. Several of the cities destroyed under Joshua were military outposts and contained few civilians. Other instances of battles may have been described in military/political language that intentionally exaggerated the action and the results, perhaps to intimidate remaining peoples or to support the status of the leaders.

Regardless of the size of the remaining Canaanite population, the threat of their cultural influence remained. Their gods included Baal and the Ashtoreths (Judges 2:13). Worship of these nature and fertility gods commonly included temple prostitution and even some child sacrifice. God eventually brought judgment to bear against Israel for following such vile rituals simply to ensure rain for good crops.

INTERESTING THOUGHTS SPARKED BY OTHERS IN MY GROUP:

Can these situations be reconciled, or must we just live with the tension? Whichever you choose, how do we do that?

GOING DEEPER

Being vulnerable is rarely easy, especially with people you don't know very well. You might be surprised to find that your openness in sharing gives others around you the courage to be open as well. All of us will get more out of the study if we can engage in honest, heartfelt conversation. So stretch yourself. It's okay to go outside your comfort zone.

GROWING

Survey your relationships, past and present, and examine how they have affected your walk with God.

Has God ever asked you to give up a relationship for the sake of your own growth and faith? Explain.

Write those reflections here.

After completing this lesson, are there any current relationships you feel should be changed?

Record your thoughts here.

LESSON 8: WHY DOES GOD USE TRAGEDY AS PART OF HIS PLAN?

GREETING

HELLO, OUR COMMUNITY IS...

How easy or difficult was it to find your three commonalities with the new group member? Any differences from the first time you did it?

PARTICIPANT GUIDE

For those of you who were the "new" person in the group, how did you feel about the change and the attempt to find three things in common with an existing group?

What kind of real-life scenarios do we know that involve similar experiences, such as loss, relocation, and identity crisis?

GROUNDING

BEHIND THE SCENES

The story of Ruth begins and ends in the little town of Bethlehem, which many people know as the birthplace of Jesus. Bethlehem means "house of bread." The first mention of it in the Bible is when Rachel died giving birth to Benjamin while she, her husband, Jacob, and their family were traveling from Bethel to Bethlehem (Genesis 35:19). So Bethlehem was an old, well-established town by the time the story of Ruth takes place. Ruth eventually married Boaz, a Jewish native of Bethlehem. Their son, Obed, became the grandfather of David (Ruth 4:22), who was anointed king of Israel by the prophet Samuel (1 Samuel 16). Prophecy pointed to the Messiah, which means "anointed one," being born through David's lineage (Jeremiah 23:5) and being born in Bethlehem (Micah 5:2).

God's Word: Ruth 1:6-18

[6] When Naomi heard in Moab that the Lord had come to the aid of his people by providing food for them, she and her daughters-in-law prepared to return home from there. [7] With her two daughters-in-law she left the place where she had been living and set out on the road that would take them back to the land of Judah.

[8] Then Naomi said to her two daughters-in-law, "Go back, each of you, to your mother's home. May the Lord show you kindness, as you have shown kindness to your dead husbands and to me. [9] May the Lord grant that each of you will find rest in the home of another husband."

Then she kissed them goodbye and they wept aloud [10] and said to her, "We will go back with you to your people."

[11] But Naomi said, "Return home, my daughters. Why would you come with me? Am I going to have any more sons, who could become your husbands? [12] Return home, my daughters; I am too old to have another husband. Even if I thought there was still hope for me—even if I had a husband tonight and then gave birth to sons—[13] would you wait until they grew up? Would you remain unmarried for them? No, my daughters. It is more bitter for me than for you, because the Lord's hand has turned against me!"

[14] At this they wept aloud again. Then Orpah kissed her mother-in-law goodbye, but Ruth clung to her.

[15] "Look," said Naomi, "your sister-in-law is going back to her people and her gods. Go back with her."

[16] But Ruth replied, "Don't urge me to leave you or to turn back from you. Where you go I will go, and where you stay I will stay. Your people will be my people and your God my God. [17] Where you die I will die, and there I will be buried. May the Lord deal with me, be it ever so severely, if even death separates you and me." [18] When Naomi realized that Ruth was determined to go with her, she stopped urging her.

What impressions or questions immediately come to mind? What words describe your reaction to this passage?

Jot down your initial thoughts here.

GRAPPLING

BEHIND THE SCENES

In the Ancient Near East, including the Israelite culture, women were typically dependent upon their male relatives for nurture, care, and support. Widows were especially vulnerable if they could not remarry, for they had no means of self-support in a male-dominated society—unless they became a beggar, prostitute, or slave.

The trio of widowed women, Naomi, Ruth, and Orpah, offered each other mutual support and encouragement. When Naomi tried to release her daughters-in-law from their responsibility to her, she was sacrificing her future to improve theirs.

List the tragedies and troubles encountered by Naomi and her daughters-in-law. What were the prospects facing widows in that culture and in those situations? How many different facets of life were affected (social, economic, spiritual, etc.)?

What emotions can you imagine Naomi feeling through her experiences of loss and change?

Why do you think Naomi's daughters-in-law started to emigrate from Moab to Bethlehem with her? What would be the pros and cons of their initial decision to leave their homeland and families of origin?

After they had started toward Bethlehem, Naomi changed her mind and tried to convince Orpah and Ruth to return to their homes in Moab (verses 8-14). How do you explain each woman's decision at this point in the story?

BEHIND THE SCENES

Naomi's sons' marriages to Moabite women were contrary to the Jewish law forbidding marriage to women from nations who served other gods. This apparently wasn't a problem in Moab, but when Naomi decided to return to Bethlehem after her sons died, it could have been a problem for her daughters-in-law. It was unlikely any man in Bethlehem would marry Ruth or Orpah. Their best option for marriage and children was to remain in Moab, return to their mothers' homes, and find husbands in their own communities. This makes Ruth's decision to follow Naomi to Bethlehem an extraordinarily courageous one.

GOING DEEPER

We've learned we can find similarities with others, but we can find differences as well. As we continue to discuss, keep in mind we process differently. We bring different experiences and priorities with us. Some people like to share a lot, and others want to quietly reflect. We have different questions and will process in different ways. Through our differences we can learn from each other. Let's open our eyes and hearts and pay attention to everyone around us. We'll learn from each other as we ask questions and respectfully share.

BEHIND THE SCENES

When Ruth followed Naomi to Bethlehem, she also committed herself to follow Israel's one true God. The name by which Ruth called God is Yahweh, which means "I am." This name was first used when God spoke to Moses in Exodus 3. *Yahweh* signifies the full presence of the eternal, sovereign God—the same God who made covenants with Naomi's ancestors, Abraham and Moses. They, too, followed God into an unfamiliar land, trusting him to provide. The vow Ruth took to follow Naomi and leave behind her own people, heritage, and god uses the same type of covenant language (Exodus 6:7; Leviticus 26:12). This radical commitment to Naomi, her people, and her God places Ruth among the greatest heroes of the Old Testament story.

INTERESTING THOUGHTS SPARKED BY OTHERS IN MY GROUP:

BEHIND THE SCENES

The religious context Ruth left behind in Moab was a far cry from the Israelite religion she adopted when she followed Naomi to Bethlehem. The Moabites worshipped the god Chemosh, who seems to be related to Molek, the god of the Ammonites. Some evidence exists that Chemosh and Molek were different names for the same god or were two manifestations of the same god. Molek is notorious for the frequency of human sacrifice in his cult, and some ancient references associate that with Chemosh, as well. Both the Moabites and Ammonites were descended from the incestuous relationship between Lot and his daughters (Genesis 19:30-38), so it makes sense that their gods would be similar. One ancient inscription identifies Chemosh with Ashtar, another Middle-East god. Ashtar (or Ishtar, or Astarte, or Ashtoreth) was a well-known fertility god or goddess, whose worshippers often practiced sacred prostitution and other sexual rites. Ironically, Solomon, Ruth's great-great-grandson, married many foreign women and introduced their foreign gods throughout his reign. First Kings 11:1-8, 33 mentions all three of these deities as having worship sites in Solomon's kingdom.

GROWING

Make a list of tragedies that you, or people you personally know, have had to endure.

Write those here.

What could you do in the next few weeks and months to prepare yourself for responding faithfully and honestly to God when tragedy befalls you?

Record those thoughts here.

How could you help support other people who are currently going through tragedy and hard times in their lives?

Write your ideas here.

LESSON 9: ARE MY ACTIONS ALONE ENOUGH TO LET OTHERS KNOW I'M A CHRISTIAN?

GREETING

What words do you and your group members think characterize each item in the list below?

- money
- car
- politician
- weather
- me
- coffee
- pets
- church
- television
- mail
- social media
- God

P A R T I C I P A N T   G U I D E

If you could describe the experience you just had, again using only one word, what would that word be?

How much easier would it be to communicate if you could add actions or demonstrations to your one word?

GROUNDING

God's Word: Ruth 2:1-13

[1] Now Naomi had a relative on her husband's side, a man of standing from the clan of Elimelek, whose name was Boaz.

[2] And Ruth the Moabite said to Naomi, "Let me go to the fields and pick up the leftover grain behind anyone in whose eyes I find favor."

Naomi said to her, "Go ahead, my daughter." [3] So she went out, entered a field and began to glean behind the harvesters. As it turned out, she was working in a field belonging to Boaz, who was from the clan of Elimelek.

[4] Just then Boaz arrived from Bethlehem and greeted the harvesters, "The Lord be with you!"

"The Lord bless you!" they answered.

[5] Boaz asked the overseer of his harvesters, "Who does that young woman belong to?"

[6] The overseer replied, "She is the Moabite who came back from Moab with Naomi. [7] She said, 'Please let me glean and gather among the

sheaves behind the harvesters.' She came into the field and has remained here from morning till now, except for a short rest in the shelter."

[8] So Boaz said to Ruth, "My daughter, listen to me. Don't go and glean in another field and don't go away from here. Stay here with the women who work for me. [9] Watch the field where the men are harvesting, and follow along after the women. I have told the men not to lay a hand on you. And whenever you are thirsty, go and get a drink from the water jars the men have filled."

[10] At this, she bowed down with her face to the ground. She asked him, "Why have I found such favor in your eyes that you notice me—a foreigner?"

[11] Boaz replied, "I've been told all about what you have done for your mother-in-law since the death of your husband—how you left your father and mother and your homeland and came to live with a people you did not know before. [12] May the Lord repay you for what you have done. May you be richly rewarded by the Lord, the God of Israel, under whose wings you have come to take refuge."

[13] "May I continue to find favor in your eyes, my lord," she said. "You have put me at ease by speaking kindly to your servant—though I do not have the standing of one of your servants."

What are your initial thoughts as you hear this part of Ruth and Boaz's story? What observations and questions immediately come to mind?

Write down your questions or thoughts here.

BEHIND THE SCENES

Ruth offered to glean, or pick up the leftover grain, in a farmer's field because she knew Israelite farmers were required to leave behind grain to provide for people. "When you reap the harvest of your land, do not reap to the very edges of your field or gather the gleanings of your harvest. Do not go over your vineyard a second time or pick up the grapes that have fallen. Leave them for the poor and the foreigner. I am the Lord your God" (Leviticus 19:9-10). In addition to the edges that were left unharvested for people in need, people like Ruth could follow the harvesters and pick up anything they had missed throughout the rest of the field.

GRAPPLING

GOING DEEPER

Like Boaz, we can be respectful even when we find differences among our experiences and opinions. In fact, we can have richer conversations because of our differences. As we continue to discuss, let's commit to respecting each other. Whether we have different perspectives or ways of sharing them, we can open our minds and hearts to consider what God wants to teach us as we ask questions, share, and grow together.

BEHIND THE SCENES

Boaz is referred to as a relative of Naomi's husband, Elimelek. However, they might not have been related as closely as we assume when we use the word "relative." Men of the same clan were assumed to have a relationship as close as relatives even when they were not related by blood. Because their clan is identified as Elimelek's, he likely had a prominent position in the clan, perhaps due to his wealth. Whether or not Boaz knew him personally, Boaz would have respected Elimelek because of his position. Relative or not, Boaz was not the person most closely connected to Elimelek, because another man had a right to marry into his family through Ruth (Ruth 3:12). Boaz was close enough to Elimelek's family that Naomi knew he was a family redeemer, although nothing is mentioned about any personal interaction between them when she first returned to Bethlehem (Ruth 2:20).

What does Boaz do and say that points to his belief and trust in God?

How do you see belief and trust in God being displayed by other people in these verses?

BEHIND THE SCENES

Boaz reveals his respect in several ways. First, he greets his workers in the Lord's name. He is not a harsh landowner whose workers are considered to only be worth their workload; Boaz's workers are treated with respect and appreciation. Second, he asks about Ruth regarding her relationships. He is not simply curious about who she is but also how she fits into existing relationships with people he might know, showing his respect for community. Finally, Boaz speaks to Ruth with respect and abundantly provides for her. He was generous far beyond his requirement by law. Boaz repeatedly uses the Lord's name and identifies God as the motivation and provider of his kindness.

How can what others say and do point us toward or away from God?

How does what *you* say and do point others toward or away from God?

INTERESTING THOUGHTS SPARKED BY OTHERS IN MY GROUP:

GROWING

BEHIND THE SCENES

The book of Ruth is read during the Jewish festival of Shavuot, also known as the Feast of Weeks or Festival of First Fruits. It coincides with the Christian celebration of Pentecost. Because Shavuot is a harvest festival, the book of Ruth is a fitting reading as it focuses on the harvest and the blessings God pours onto the poor and abandoned. The reading also commemorates the life and death of David, who tradition says was born and died around the same time as Shavuot. Ruth was David's great-grandmother. Jesus was born through David's lineage. In addition, many Jewish boys and girls in their early teens confirm their commitment to their faith during this festival time, reflecting Ruth's commitment to follow Yahweh, the Lord of Israel.

What is one step you believe God is prompting you to take that would help you trust him more?

Write your idea here.

As you talk with your group, write people's commitments here as a reminder to encourage them in the coming days and weeks.

Write those here.

P A R T I C I P A N T   G U I D E

LESSON 9: ARE MY ACTIONS ALONE ENOUGH TO **69**
LET OTHERS KNOW I'M A CHRISTIAN?

LESSON 10: WHAT IS A REDEEMER, AND WHAT DOES THIS HAVE TO DO WITH ME TODAY?

GREETING

What has been the most significant purchase you have ever made for yourself? You don't need to divulge any money amounts. In fact, the most significant purchase may not have been the most expensive, but the most meaningful. Describe what you purchased and what made it such a big deal at the time.

What's the most significant purchase you've ever made for someone else?

Have you ever been the recipient of another person's generosity in a big way? If so, what was that experience like?

GROUNDING

BEHIND THE SCENES

This passage mentions an unnamed man who was the guardian-redeemer for Naomi and Ruth. Other Bible translations call him a family guardian or kinsman-redeemer. This description comes from the Hebrew word *go'el*, meaning "redeemer." A go'el was a male relative who was responsible for caring for a deceased relative's possessions, including land, houses, livestock, and even the widow. If the deceased had debts, the go'el would pay them. If the deceased was childless, the go'el would marry the widow and produce offspring who would carry on the name and family lineage of the deceased man. When they came of age, those children would inherit the deceased man's property. The possessions and people who were cared for by a go'el were said to be "redeemed."

The go'el's responsibility, then, was supremely sacrificial: He invested much in supporting his deceased relative's estate and family but received little to nothing in return. Israel's social system and survival as a people depended on men who performed their duty as a go'el. So important was this role that Isaiah 43:14 describes God as Israel's go'el or redeemer, a concept that carries over to the New Testament understanding of Jesus' life and ministry.

God's Word: Ruth 4:1-12

[1] Meanwhile Boaz went up to the town gate and sat down there just as the guardian-redeemer he had mentioned came along. Boaz said, "Come over here, my friend, and sit down." So he went over and sat down.

[2] Boaz took ten of the elders of the town and said, "Sit here," and they did so. [3] Then he said to the guardian-redeemer, "Naomi, who has come back from Moab, is selling the piece of land that belonged to our relative Elimelek. [4] I thought I should bring the matter to your attention and suggest that you buy it in the presence of these seated here and in the presence of the elders of my people. If you will redeem it, do so. But if you will not, tell me, so I will know. For no one has the right to do it except you, and I am next in line."

"I will redeem it," he said.

[5] Then Boaz said, "On the day you buy the land from Naomi, you also acquire Ruth the Moabite, the dead man's widow, in order to maintain the name of the dead with his property."

[6] At this, the guardian-redeemer said, "Then I cannot redeem it because I might endanger my own estate. You redeem it yourself. I cannot do it."

[7] (Now in earlier times in Israel, for the redemption and transfer of property to become final, one party took off his sandal and gave it to the other. This was the method of legalizing transactions in Israel.)

[8] So the guardian-redeemer said to Boaz, "Buy it yourself." And he removed his sandal.

[9] Then Boaz announced to the elders and all the people, "Today you are witnesses that I have bought from Naomi all the property of Elimelek, Kilion and Mahlon. [10] I have also acquired Ruth the Moabite, Mahlon's widow, as my wife, in order to maintain the name of the dead with his property, so that his name will not disappear from among his family or from his hometown. Today you are witnesses!"

¹¹ Then the elders and all the people at the gate said, "We are witnesses. May the Lord make the woman who is coming into your home like Rachel and Leah, who together built up the family of Israel. May you have standing in Ephrathah and be famous in Bethlehem. ¹² Through the offspring the Lord gives you by this young woman, may your family be like that of Perez, whom Tamar bore to Judah."

What went through your mind as you read this account? What questions come to mind? What impressions of Boaz did you get?

Jot your initial thoughts and questions here.

BEHIND THE SCENES

Boaz was a well-to-do farmer who owned land and crops and had numerous employees. Why would he be interested in a poor Moabite widow such as Ruth, despite Jewish law forbidding intermarriage with Moabites? It so happens that Boaz was a fifth generation descendant of Perez, who was the son of a Canaanite widow named Tamar. Tamar's first two husbands died. They were both sons of Judah, one of the great-grandsons of Abraham himself, the father of the Jewish people. Judah promised to give her his third son, but he neglected to fulfill that promise. So Tamar used some loopholes in the law, plus a little trickery, to get Judah to father twin sons, one of whom was named Perez. (Genesis 38 has the full details.) Thus, Tamar provided for her future security and family line. Perhaps this was why Boaz was sensitive to the plight of disadvantaged foreign widows such as Ruth. And he was brave enough to ignore social stigma to follow through on his promises to care for her.

$\checkmark$GRAPPLING

What do you think about the guardian-redeemer system at work in this story? What modern customs or laws do we have that have similar goals?

Regarding the business deal Boaz made with Ruth's guardian-redeemer, what were the costs and benefits for Boaz? What were the costs and benefits for Ruth?

BEHIND THE SCENES

Boaz met the unnamed man who was entitled to be Ruth's guardian-redeemer at the town gate. This setting is significant, for that was where officials handled town business and where private business deals were legalized. As romantic as parts of the book of Ruth sound to us today, Boaz was there strictly on business. Women were considered in the same category as land or livestock when it came to transferring ownership or responsibility for them. They were part of a man's household with no legal rights to their own property.

Because such a legal proceeding required witnesses, Boaz made sure elders were present. His business was two-fold: 1) to transfer ownership—or redemption—of Elimelek's land; 2) to ensure that Elimelek's family name would continue through Ruth, the only childbearing female of his household. Any offspring would inherit Elimelek's property and carry on his family name. The possibility of a mixed-race child taking over the land was a complication the guardian-redeemer didn't want. The matter was settled as he gave his sandal to Boaz, a gesture that was already archaic at the time. The way was clear for Boaz to become Ruth's guardian-redeemer.

If Boaz already had land and wealth and any land he purchased from Naomi would go to Ruth's future son, why do you think he chose to become Ruth's guardian-redeemer?

Boaz and Ruth had a son, Obed, who was an ancestor of King David and, by extension, Jesus. How has Jesus functioned as a guardian-redeemer for us, like Boaz did for Ruth and Naomi?

GOING DEEPER

This is a safe place where we welcome sharing. We can respect each other even when we have differences of opinions. Our different personalities, experiences, and perspectives can enrich our conversations. Let's open our ears and hearts to listen to what God wants us to learn through others and his Word.

INTERESTING THOUGHTS SPARKED BY OTHERS IN MY GROUP:

PARTICIPANT GUIDE

GROWING

BEHIND THE SCENES

The Hebrew word for *redeem* is used 22 times in Ruth and 104 times throughout the Old Testament. It means to restore, repair, or avenge. God is the ultimate redeemer (Isaiah 49:26). In the Old Testament, God redeemed people from slavery (Exodus 6:6), disobedience (Isaiah 44:22), harm (Genesis 48:16), enemies (Psalm 107:2), captivity (Isaiah 43:14), and death (Hosea 13:14). In the New Testament, God sent Jesus to provide redemption for all people: "All have sinned and fall short of the glory of God, and all are justified freely by his grace through the redemption that came by Christ Jesus" (Romans 3:23-24).

What are some ways we might express our gratitude for God's redemptive actions for us?

Record those ideas here.

How might *we* function to guard or redeem someone in our sphere of influence?

Write those thoughts here.

What might it cost us, and are we willing to pay that cost?

Add those ideas here.

LESSON 11: WHEN IS IT OKAY TO HIDE MY FAITH?

GREETING

What's your opinion of masquerade parties or other events at which you are disguised in some sort of costume? What is the reason for your opinion?

P A R T I C I P A N T   G U I D E

GROUNDING

God's Word: Esther 2:8-20

[8] When the king's order and edict had been proclaimed, many young women were brought to the citadel of Susa and put under the care of Hegai. Esther also was taken to the king's palace and entrusted to Hegai, who had charge of the harem. [9] She pleased him and won his favor. Immediately he provided her with her beauty treatments and special food. He assigned to her seven female attendants selected from the king's palace and moved her and her attendants into the best place in the harem.

[10] Esther had not revealed her nationality and family background, because Mordecai had forbidden her to do so. [11] Every day he walked back and forth near the courtyard of the harem to find out how Esther was and what was happening to her.

[12] Before a young woman's turn came to go in to King Xerxes, she had to complete twelve months of beauty treatments prescribed for the women, six months with oil of myrrh and six with perfumes and cosmetics. [13] And this is how she would go to the king: Anything she wanted was given her to take with her from the harem to the king's palace. [14] In the evening she would go there and in the morning return to another part of the harem to the care of Shaashgaz, the king's eunuch who was in charge of the concubines. She would not return to the king unless he was pleased with her and summoned her by name.

[15] When the turn came for Esther (the young woman Mordecai had adopted, the daughter of his uncle Abihail) to go to the king, she asked for nothing other than what Hegai, the king's eunuch who was in charge of the harem, suggested. And Esther won the favor of everyone who saw her. [16] She was taken to King Xerxes in the royal residence in the tenth month, the month of Tebeth, in the seventh year of his reign.

▶

[17] Now the king was attracted to Esther more than to any of the other women, and she won his favor and approval more than any of the other virgins. So he set a royal crown on her head and made her queen instead of Vashti. [18] And the king gave a great banquet, Esther's banquet, for all his nobles and officials. He proclaimed a holiday throughout the provinces and distributed gifts with royal liberality.

[19] When the virgins were assembled a second time, Mordecai was sitting at the king's gate. [20] But Esther had kept secret her family background and nationality just as Mordecai had told her to do, for she continued to follow Mordecai's instructions as she had done when he was bringing her up.

What went through your mind as you read this account? What questions came to mind?

Write your initial thoughts and questions here.

BEHIND THE SCENES

The name *Esther* is Persian in origin and means "star," while her Hebrew name, *Hadassah*, means "myrtle." The name *Mordecai* is also Persian and is connected to the name of the god Marduk; we don't know his Hebrew name. In the Hebrew Bible they are both known by their Persian names, as are the well-known trio of Jews who were taken from their home 150 years earlier, Shadrach, Meshach, and Abednego.

GRAPPLING

GOING DEEPER

You can help others in your group go deeper by listening with your full attention and by asking questions as others share. Saying "I wonder about what you just said. Tell me more!" will help people know you care about what they're saying and want them to open up more.

BEHIND THE SCENES

The events in Esther take place approximately 115 years after Nebuchadnezzar overthrew Jerusalem and took the first wave of Jewish captives to Babylon. Sixty years later, the Persian king Cyrus overthrew Babylon and decreed the Jews should be allowed to return to Jerusalem. While as many as 50,000 did return, not all Jews left the Persian Empire. Esther's family were some who did not return to Jerusalem but stayed in Susa (in what is now Iran), which is where Esther lived with her older cousin, Mordecai. The Jews who did return to Jerusalem rebuilt the Temple, which you can read about in the book of Ezra.

Why do you think Mordecai instructed Esther to keep her religion and ethnic identity hidden from King Xerxes and his officials?

What did she have to gain by doing so?

What did she have to lose if she *didn't* follow Mordecai's instructions?

BEHIND THE SCENES

The book of Esther gives us little information about Esther and Mordecai's life before Esther enters the king's palace as a contestant in the "Who's Going to Be the Next Queen?" pageant. As a result, scholars do not agree on the character of Esther and Mordecai's faith. Some propose they were true to their Jewish faith and belief in God, while others point to Esther's willingness to not observe Jewish feasts, to marry outside her faith, and to eat nonkosher food as indications that she was not closely following Jewish tradition and law. Additionally, both Esther and Mordecai were not using their Hebrew names but Persian names, which would allow them to blend in with their culture. It appears that Esther wasn't just keeping her faith secret from King Xerxes, but from everyone.

Do you think Esther had fully assimilated to the Persian culture? Or was she merely adapting some external parts of Persian culture in order to get along?

It's interesting to note that God is never mentioned in the book of Esther. How might God's "hiddenness" be reflected in Esther hiding her Jewish identity?

What lessons might we take from this passage about how we are to live and talk about our Christian faith?

> ## INTERESTING THOUGHTS SPARKED BY OTHERS IN MY GROUP:

BEHIND THE SCENES

Esther is not the only biblical figure who kept their faith a secret. In John 3 we see Nicodemus, an influential Pharisee, coming to meet with Jesus in secret, and again in chapter 7, he defends Jesus against the Sanhedrin. Later, in chapter 19, he appears again with Joseph of Arimathea, who "was a disciple of Jesus, but secretly because he feared the Jewish leaders." Both of these men, who struggled with making their faith public, had the honor of taking the body of Jesus from the cross, preparing it for burial, and placing him in the tomb.

GROWING

Is my faith something I hide out of fear of rejection, or apathy, or have I carefully discerned how to live and speak about faith?

Write your reflection here.

In what ways does my life proclaim my faith in Christ, even if I don't use words? Are there any changes I would like to make?

Write those ideas here.

LESSON 12: HOW FAR SHOULD I GO TO RIGHT A WRONG?

GREETING

If you could travel back in time to any historic event, what would you choose? Why?

Imagine your time machine has arrived in Nazi-occupied Holland in 1942. You cannot leave for at least one year. You must choose, as a group of four, one of three options: 1) you can be an observer of all that happens; 2) you can live with a family who is hiding Jews; 3) you can become a collaborator with the Nazi police force in that town.

Which would be the safest choice?

Which option will your group choose, and why?

GROUNDING

God's Word: Esther 4:8-17

[8] He also gave him a copy of the text of the edict for their annihilation, which had been published in Susa, to show to Esther and explain it to her, and he told him to instruct her to go into the king's presence to beg for mercy and plead with him for her people.

[9] Hathak went back and reported to Esther what Mordecai had said. [10] Then she instructed him to say to Mordecai, [11] "All the king's officials and the people of the royal provinces know that for any man or woman who approaches the king in the inner court without being summoned the king has but one law: that they be put to death unless the king extends the gold scepter to them and spares their lives. But thirty days have passed since I was called to go to the king."

[12] When Esther's words were reported to Mordecai, [13] he sent back this answer: "Do not think that because you are in the king's house you alone of all the Jews will escape. [14] For if you remain silent at this time, relief and deliverance for the Jews will arise from another place, but you and your father's family will perish. And who knows but that you have come to your royal position for such a time as this?"

[15] Then Esther sent this reply to Mordecai: [16] "Go, gather together all the Jews who are in Susa, and fast for me. Do not eat or drink for three days, night or day. I and my attendants will fast as you do. When this is done, I will go to the king, even though it is against the law. And if I perish, I perish."

[17] So Mordecai went away and carried out all of Esther's instructions.

What went through your mind as you read this account? Is there something here you question?

Write your initial thoughts and questions here.

BEHIND THE SCENES

Esther's fear of Xerxes was not unfounded. Just a few years earlier he had replaced Queen Vashti for refusing to come when called. What might happen if Esther came *without* being called?

King Xerxes had a reputation for acting rashly and in anger. The historian Herodotus related an incident in which Xerxes had commanded a bridge to be built over the Hellespont (now called the Dardanelles in modern Turkey). Just as the bridge was completed, a storm arose and ruined the bridge. Xerxes, in a rage, commanded that the Hellespont receive 300 lashes and beheaded the men who were responsible for building the bridge.

Clearly Esther didn't have a close relationship with the king, and his reaction to her sudden appearance at the throne room was something she could not predict. Her dilemma was certainly a real one that could cost Esther her life and not save anyone.

GRAPPLING

GOING DEEPER

Esther's courage in approaching the king with her plea for her people is a great example for all of us. In the course of your conversations during this lesson, there may be opportunity for your group members to tell their own stories of facing religious persecution or discrimination. Although one person's definition of "persecution" may differ from yours, be a patient listener, for no one can know how difficult it may be for another person to demonstrate courage in situations they perceive as personally threatening.

BEHIND THE SCENES

During Esther's time, the gate of the city, also known as the King's Gate, was a busy place where trade and judicial matters were transacted and important announcements were made. Mordecai's presence at the King's Gate indicates that he held a place of some importance. While it's not clear what position he held (some have suggested he was a doorkeeper, while others have proposed he worked within the judicial system), it is clear this was a place he frequented and was known by the king's officials there.

In verse 8, Mordecai urges Esther to go to the king to plead for her people. This would require her to reveal her Jewish identity. In chapter 2, Mordecai instructed her to keep her identity hidden. Why the change of mind?

Esther at first hesitated to follow Mordecai's strategy to go to the king. What would you have done in her place, and why?

BEHIND THE SCENES

In Esther 4:1 we read that Mordecai tore his clothes, put on sackcloth and ashes, and went wailing through the city. The man who previously hid his Jewish heritage is now making it known in an act that shouts of humility and repentance: mourning. Jews throughout the king's province joined him in covering themselves in sackcloth and ashes, "fasting, weeping and wailing." After learning the impending fate of her people, Esther begins her own fast, recruiting all Jews in Susa, as well as her own maids, to join her. With all this mourning, fasting, and wailing, you might notice that the book of Esther never mentions that she, or Mordecai, ever prayed. Other Scripture related to this general time period shows a correlation between praying and fasting (Ezra 10:1, Nehemiah 1:4). It may be assumed that Esther, Mordecai, and the Jews of the province didn't simply abstain from eating but went to God to help them right this horrible wrong.

In verse 14, Mordecai states that rescue for the Jews will come from some source, whether Esther goes to the king or not. What does this imply about human free will and some overarching plan or purpose?

Mordecai's question of whether Esther may have become queen "for such a time as this" seems to imply some greater purpose, perhaps referring to God. How can we know whether or not God is involved in the details of human history and to what degree?

When Esther resolved to go to the king, she said, "And if I perish, I perish." How would you interpret Esther's attitude here? Resignation to fate? Selfless bravery? Other?

INTERESTING THOUGHTS SPARKED BY OTHERS IN
MY GROUP:

GROWING

In her book *The Hiding Place*, Corrie Ten Boom retells an incident that occurred in Holland prior to her imprisonment during World War II. A local pastor had refused to hide a Jewish baby for fear of losing his life. Corrie's father took the baby and said, "You say that we could lose our lives for this child. I would consider that the greatest honor that could come to my family."

Where might this type of selflessness be seen today?

Write your ideas here.

BEHIND THE SCENES

The Bible is full of seemingly unimportant people doing seemingly unimportant things but whose presence makes a world of difference. The story of Esther is no different, as each character is simply a person doing what's been put before them.

Esther: an orphan girl who gets caught up in a politically required beauty pageant and becomes queen. Mordecai: the uncle who refuses to kneel out of his own conviction and ends up starting a war. Hathak: a servant who shuttles important messages between the queen and her uncle... messages that change the queen and affect the lives of untold numbers.

What is the purpose and effect of group fasting? Would our group or church ever attempt to do something like this?

Write your thoughts here.

What current issue or event is worth mourning, repenting, and fasting?

Record those thoughts here.

What situation or issue could I help with but that will require some courage on my part? Is there a relationship that needs mending, breaking, or being honest about? Is there an action I need to take at work? What cost am I willing to pay?

Write your reflections here.

LESSON 13: HOW DO I KNOW GOD IS IN CONTROL?

GREETING

What do cinnamon sticks, goldfish, keys, and acorns have in common?

GROUNDING

God's Word: Esther 7

[1] So the king and Haman went to Queen Esther's banquet, [2] and as they were drinking wine on the second day, the king again asked, "Queen Esther, what is your petition? It will be given you. What is your request? Even up to half the kingdom, it will be granted."

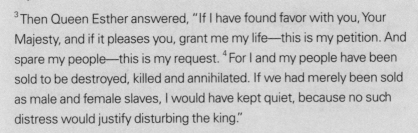

³ Then Queen Esther answered, "If I have found favor with you, Your Majesty, and if it pleases you, grant me my life—this is my petition. And spare my people—this is my request. ⁴ For I and my people have been sold to be destroyed, killed and annihilated. If we had merely been sold as male and female slaves, I would have kept quiet, because no such distress would justify disturbing the king."

⁵ King Xerxes asked Queen Esther, "Who is he? Where is he—the man who has dared to do such a thing?"

⁶ Esther said, "An adversary and enemy! This vile Haman!"

Then Haman was terrified before the king and queen. ⁷ The king got up in a rage, left his wine and went out into the palace garden. But Haman, realizing that the king had already decided his fate, stayed behind to beg Queen Esther for his life.

⁸ Just as the king returned from the palace garden to the banquet hall, Haman was falling on the couch where Esther was reclining.

The king exclaimed, "Will he even molest the queen while she is with me in the house?"

As soon as the word left the king's mouth, they covered Haman's face. ⁹ Then Harbona, one of the eunuchs attending the king, said, "A pole reaching to a height of fifty cubits stands by Haman's house. He had it set up for Mordecai, who spoke up to help the king."

The king said, "Impale him on it!" ¹⁰ So they impaled Haman on the pole he had set up for Mordecai. Then the king's fury subsided.

What went through your mind as you read this account? What impressions did you get? Is there something here you question?

Write down your thoughts, observations, and questions here.

GRAPPLING

What do you think of Esther and her strategy for asking King Xerxes to save the Jewish people? What, if anything, would you have done differently?

Who do you credit most for saving the Jews from Haman's vile plot? Esther, Mordecai, Xerxes, luck, fate, or God?

There is no explicit mention of God in the book of Esther, but some people claim that God's activity can be seen in the background of the events described there. What is your opinion? What do you see in this text or the book of Esther as a whole to support your opinion? What other parts of Scripture support your opinion?

BEHIND THE SCENES

Banquets are a big part of the plot in the book of Esther. There are seven banquets total within the 10 chapters that comprise Esther. This is not unusual for ancient Persia. Banquets were a time not only of celebrating but for decision making and religious ceremonies. Did you notice the length of Xerxes's first banquet? 180 days! It's possible this elaborate banquet was used as a time to plan Xerxes's military invasion of Greece in 481 B.C. The banquet Esther held is called a "banquet of wine" in some versions of the Bible. It was not unusual for wine to be the centerpiece of a banquet in ancient Persia. Archeologists have discovered jars from 4000 B.C. (well before Esther) containing wine residue, and it was well known during the time of Esther that the Persians were fond of wine. They believed it was good practice to make important decisions when drunk, as this is when the truth will be told. This makes Esther's banquet all the more understandable, as she uses this banquet of wine to disclose her Jewish lineage and Haman's plot to destroy her people.

A popular saying is that "hindsight is 20-20." How does the passage of time affect our view of God's role in human events and experiences?

BEHIND THE SCENES

Three different versions of Esther have been found, one written in Hebrew and two in Greek. The Hebrew version is the one found in Protestant Bibles and does not include prayer or the name of God anywhere. The Greek version is very similar to the Hebrew, but it includes six additions that are prayers or prophetic visions. This is the version that is included in Roman Catholic and Eastern Orthodox Bibles. The additional passages are short, but they make a huge difference in the message of Esther.

There has been great debate throughout the centuries as to whether Esther should have been included in the Bible at all due to its lack of spiritual content. But historically, the Jewish faith has always considered it inspired by God and accepted as Scripture.

INTERESTING THOUGHTS SPARKED BY OTHERS IN MY GROUP:

PARTICIPANT GUIDE

GOING DEEPER

This lesson may challenge your worldview. Some people and Christian traditions seek to find natural or logical ways to describe how God works in the world. (Using modern astronomy to explain the phenomenon of the star of Bethlehem, for example.) Others are perfectly comfortable living with divine mystery and seeing all of creation infused with God's presence and activity.

Wherever you find yourself on that spectrum, you will benefit from looking at things from new or different perspectives. Try to be open to seeing the world as others in your group or class do. Spiritual maturity depends on this kind of openness. Regardless of how successful you are in doing this, be sure you leave room for others to express their opinions and beliefs in a safe and non-condemning atmosphere.

GROWING

BEHIND THE SCENES

Haman's fate is both ironic and gruesome. He was humiliated in chapter 6 when the king directed him to lead the parade honoring Mordecai, whom Haman had planned to personally execute as part of his plot to murder all the Jews in Persia. When Queen Esther revealed that plot to the king in chapter 7, the king left the banquet room in an angry fit. In a last-ditch effort to save himself, Haman threw himself on Esther's dining couch to beg for mercy. In doing so, he forgot the royal protocol of never being alone with the king's wife or concubines. When the king returned and saw Haman so near the queen, Haman's fate was sealed. ▶

The manner of Haman's execution is debatable. Some Bible translations say he was hanged on the gallows he had built for Mordecai. Other versions state he was impaled on a pole he had erected. The Hebrew word translates literally as "tree," which leaves the meaning open to interpretation. In light of the documented Persian use of impalement and crucifixion to execute those guilty of crimes against the state, the New International Version is probably correct in stating that Haman died by impalement.

What factors might keep us from recognizing God's grace at work in the world?

Write those ideas here.

Who or what can help us discern how (or if) God is working in the events of our lives or in the world at large?

Record those thoughts here.

PARTICIPANT GUIDE

What do you think is a balanced view of how God moves and works in our lives and in the world?

Write your response here.

How will your future decisions and actions reflect this balance?

Jot down some ideas here.

The Lord's Prayer

Our Father in heaven, hallowed be your name,
your kingdom come, your will be done,
    on earth as it is in heaven.
Give us today our daily bread.
And forgive us our debts,
    as we also have forgiven our debtors.
And lead us not into temptation, but deliver us from evil.
For yours is the kingdom and the power and the glory forever.
Amen.